G000153496

The Pillow Book ╱
By Jee Le

Published in the United States by Awai Books,
an imprint of Awai LLC. New York. 1133 Broadway.
Suite 708, New York, NY 10010

Japanese translation © 2014 Awai LLC.
Original English text © 2012 Jee Leong Koh
Translator: Keisuke Tsubono
Illustrator: Mariko Hirasawa
Art Director: C. Xiroh

Note that Math Paper Press published the first
edition of The Pillow Book in Singapore and
Anna Sai illustrated its inspiring cover art.

2014 年 6 月 30 日　初版
著者　ジー・リオン・コー
訳者　坪野圭介
イラスト　平澤まりこ
デザイン　C. Xiroh
発行　Awai Books

ISBN: 978-1-937220-03-7
eISBN: 978-1-937220-04-4

www.awaimedia.com

# The Pillow Book

## by Jee Leong Koh

Translator: Keisuke Tsubono

Illustrator: Mariko Hirasawa

Awai Books

One day Lord Korechika, the Minister of the Centre, brought the Empress a bundle of notebooks. 'What shall we do with them?' Her Majesty asked me, 'The Emperor has already made arrangements for copying the "Records of the Historian".'

'Let me make them into a pillow,' I said.

'Very well,' said Her Majesty. 'You may have them.'

I now had a vast quantity of paper at my disposal, and I set about filling the notebooks with odd facts, stories from the past, and all sorts of other things, often including the most trivial material. On the whole I concentrated on things and people that I found charming and splendid; my notes are also full of poems and observations on trees and plants, birds and insects. I was sure that when people saw my book they would say, 'It's even worse than I expected. Now one can really tell what she is like.' After all, it is written entirely for my own amusement and I put things down exactly as they came to me. How could my casual jottings possibly bear comparison with the many impressive books that exist in our time?

—from *The Pillow Book* of Sei Shōnagon, translated from Japanese by Ivan Morris.

宮の御前に、内の大臣のたてまつりたまへりけるを、「これに、何を書かまし。うへの御前には、史記といふ文をなむ、書かせたまへる」など、のたまはせしを、「枕にこそは侍らめ」と申ししかば、「さば、得てよ」とて賜はせたりしを、あやしきを、「こよや」「なにや」と、つきせずおほかる紙を書きつくさんとせしに、いと物おぼえぬことぞ多かるや。

　おほかたこれは、世の中にをかしきこと、人のめでたしなど思ふべき名を選り出でて、歌などをも、木、草、鳥、虫をもいひ出したらばこそ、「思ふほどよりはわろし、心見えなり」ともそしられめ。ただ心ひとつに、おのずから思ふことを、たはぶれに書きつけたれば、「物に立ちまじり、人なみなみなるべき耳をも聞くべきものかはと思ひしに、「はづかしきなども、見る人はしたまふなれば、いとあやしうぞあるや。


（清少納言『枕草子』より）

## I MISS MY BOLSTER

I miss my bolster, the long pillow held between my legs and hugged to my chest from the time I was born to when I turned thirtythree.

I have the impression that it was the same pillow although this could not be true. Perhaps it stayed the same because the slip would change. A fresh pillowslip smelled not unpleasantly of washing powder. After drying in the sun for hours on a bamboo pole, it was hot to my thighs. I also liked the sensation of it cooling and, later at night, the sensation of warming it in the cleft of my body.

There was a dark brown pillowslip with overlapping white squares. Another pillowslip was blue with white balloons. My favorite had the pattern of palm leaves.

Darren laughed at the bolster when he visited me from England and slept in the same room. We must get you a woman, he said. Darren had straw blond hair and a swimmer's shoulders. At the beach he pulled on green shorts, the same lime green that Matt Damon flashed in *The Talented Mr. Ripley*. The color picked him out in the crowd. I mean Damon but I could have been talking about Darren.

In the year I turned thirtythree, I moved to New York City, to find out if I was gay and a poet. For the first time in my life I bought my own mattress and bed linen. I learned about sizes: full, queen, king. Mine is twin. I have two pillows for the head but none for the body. I could not find one but I admit I did not look very hard. I gave the bolster up to get something better.

## 抱き枕が恋しい

　抱き枕が恋しい。生まれてから33歳になるまで、足のあいだに挟んで、胸に抱きしめていた長い枕。

　本当かわからないけれど、ずっと同じ枕だったような気がしている。もしかしたら枕カバーが変わってきただけで、中はずっと同じだったかもしれない。洗いたての枕カバーは洗剤の心地良い香りがした。太陽の下で竹竿に何時間か干した後の枕は、太ももに触れると熱かった。それから、だんだん冷たくなっていく感覚も、夜遅くに僕のからだに挟まれてまた温かくなっていく感覚も、僕は好きだった。

　白い正方形の模様が重なり合う、ダークブラウンの枕カバー。青地に白い水玉模様のカバーもあった。僕のお気に入りは、ヤシの葉っぱ柄だった。

　ダレンがイギリスから訪ねてきて、一緒に僕の部屋に泊まったとき、彼は抱き枕のことを笑った。君に女の子を見つけてこなきゃな、と僕に言った。ダレンは麦わら色のブロンドの持ち主で、水泳選手みたいな肩をしていた。海辺では緑色の水着を身につけていた。『リプリー』の中でマット・デイモンがちらっと覗かせた水着と、まったく同じライムグリーン。人ごみの中でも、その色ですぐに彼を見つけ出せる。デイモンのことを言ったんだけど、ダレンについても同じことが言えると思う。

33歳になった年に、ニューヨークシティに引っ越した。はたして僕はゲイで詩人なのか、答えを見つけるために。人生ではじめて、自分のマットレスとシーツ類を買った。サイズについても学んだ。フルサイズ、クイーンサイズ、キングサイズ。僕のはツインだ。頭を載せる枕は二つ買ったけれど、からだ用は買わなかった。いいやつを見つけられなかったからなんだけど、必死に探そうともしなかったことは認めなきゃならない。他にもっといいものを手に入れるために、抱き枕はやめにしたんだ。

## *WHEN MY PARENTS GAVE UP THEIR IDOLS*

When my parents gave up their idols for the Christian faith, they asked a priest from the nearest temple to send the household gods off. The altars, gold calligraphy on red sheet metal, were left at the base of a rain tree. The next day they were gone.

The altar table was not so easily removed. A dour work of dark pinewood, without any charm, it had stood in the living room for as long as I could remember. We tried changing its purpose, at one time storing my trophies and plaques behind its glass. They never looked right there. After it was finally hauled away, father had to paint over the soot left by burning years of incense.

What to put in its place? My bookcase, from IKEA, sagged and leaned forward alarmingly. The corner was too small for the dining table we rediscovered every New Year's Eve when we sat together for my mother's steamboat treat. Then there were no more reunion dinners when my sister and I moved to the States. My parents changed the round table for a rectangle and jabbed it into the space.

Now the table holds boxes of tissue, biscuits soft enough for father's gums, mother's diabetes pills, and my white laptop when I visit during my summer break and wish to write.

## 両親が仏像を手放したとき

　僕の両親がキリスト教への信仰のために仏像を手放した
とき、一番近くにある寺院の住職に、家の仏具を送らせて
もらえるように頼んだ。金色の漢字が彫られた赤い金属板
の載った祭壇の経机は、家のレインツリーの根元に運ばれ
た。次の日、仏具たちは去っていった。

　その経机を持ち出すのは簡単なことじゃなかったんだ。黒
い松からつくられた陰気な物体にはなんの効験もなかったけ
れど、僕が覚えている限り、そいつはずっとリビングに置か
れていた。用途を変えてみようと、一度、ガラスの奥に僕
がもらったトロフィーや記念の盾なんかをしまってみたこ
ともある。それがふさわしいとは全然思えなかった。とう
とう机が運び去られた後には、長年焚いてきた線香によっ
て染みついた煤のせいで、父が壁を塗り直すはめになった。

　代わりにその場所に置かれたのは、僕の IKEA の本棚
だった。たわんで、危なっかしく前に傾いているやつだ。
毎年大晦日には、母のとびきりのご馳走を食べようと一
家みんなで机を囲むんだけど、そのときになって決まって
引っ張り出してくるダイニングテーブルを置くには、残り
のスペースは狭すぎた。その後、僕と妹はアメリカに引っ
越してしまったから、みんなで集まって夕飯を食べるこ
ともなくなった。両親は、丸机から長方形のものにかえ
て、結局そのスペースに無理やりテーブルを押し込んだ。

　今、そのテーブルには、ティッシュボックス、父が噛める柔ら
かいビスケット、母の糖尿病の錠剤、それから夏の休暇と執筆の
ために僕が家に戻るときには白いラップトップが置かれている。

## *WELL ORGANIZED THINGS*

A dictionary. A rainforest. A supermarket.

A columbarium, a place to urn the dead, is organized for the convenience of the living. The Civil Service, a place to earn a living, is organized for the dead.

The passport office in Singapore.

A dragonfly. A quartz.




## よく整えられた物たち

辞書。熱帯雨林。スーパーマーケット。

死者が骨を納める地下墓地は、生者の便宜のために整えられている。生者が金を納める官公庁は、死者の便宜のために整えられている。

シンガポールのパスポートオフィス。

トンボ。石英。

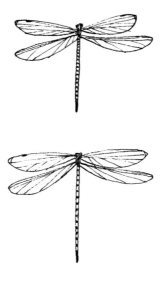

## DISORGANIZED THINGS

The Botanic Gardens after a storm. The apartment after a party.

Before the command to come to attention, the enlistees relax in various states of sleep, their rifle slings entangled with their limbs.

When I cross the checkpoint into Johor Bahru, I cannot help observing that the trees that were planted in regimental intervals now sprout in confusion. The city has poured and set round them, and not they for the city. If the trees have given the pleasure of pattern before, they now surprise with their surge of green.

Disheveled hair.

## 散らかった物たち

　嵐が去った植物園。パーティーが済んだアパートの一室。

　召集命令が下される前、志願兵たちはのびのびと様々な姿勢で眠りにつき、彼らの銃のスリングは手足に絡まりついている。

　ジョホールバルの検問所を通るとき、厳格に決められた間隔で植えられたはずの木々が今ではあちこち伸び放題になっている様子が必ず目に留まる。街が木々の周りに降り注いで勝手に固まったのであって、木々が街のために生えたわけじゃない。かつて木々がパターンの愉しみを与えてくれていたとしたら、今では緑色のうねりと共に驚きを与えてくれている。

　乱れた髪。

## MUSICAL INSTRUMENTS

On my way to hear the London Philharmonic at Lincoln Center, a woman with straggly white hair entered my train and started to play a pianica. I was instantly transported back to the music room of my primary school, where a tag of boys sat, four to a bench, fumbled on the keyboard of their instruments and blew lustily into the creamy white tubing.

In secondary school everyone learned to play the guitar. No more the small music room with its floor of flagstones, always doubling up as a passageway. The boy scouts had their own basement den, to pick up the major chords and talk about the opposite sex. Samantha, from Cedar Girls, is the only name I remember now. At the campfire, Lawrence, my patrol leader, could not stop looking at her. Pugfaced Lawrence, he flashed an uncertain temper. Once, when we messed up a backwoods dinner, he stalked over to Swift Patrol and ate with them instead. The sense of abandonment was as sharp as when father walked out of a quarrel with mother. Now married and a Brigade Commander in the army, he found the chords for 'Leader of the Band' played constantly on the radio then, and we all sang along.

There was so much singing. The Baptist hymnal, maroon cover protected by plastic, was a favorite, but when the church split up and I left with the pastor dismissed for speaking in tongues, I took to the choruses projected on the back of the stage of a rented auditorium. "Jesus, I Love You." "Jesus, Take Me As I Am." The songs were not about words or music. They were about the primitive power of repetition to reach heaven. The pastor, another Lawrence, now travels round the world, cutting up his daughter and putting her back, in a magic act.

I loved singing, and so I thought I could. Elsa, whom everyone decided sang like an angel, disabused me of that notion. Although I left the church, I may still be trying to reach a place where that notion holds true.

## 楽器

　リンカーンセンターにロンドン・フィルの演奏を聴き
にいく途中、同じ電車に乗り合わせたぼさぼさの白髪の
女性がピアニカを演奏しはじめた。たちまち僕は小学校
の音楽室へと引き戻された。名札をつけた男の子たちが
四人掛けの長椅子に座って、めいめい鍵盤を叩いたり管
楽器を思い切り吹いたりしていた場所。

　中学校では誰もがギターの弾き方を学んだ。床に敷石
の並んだ音楽室はすごく狭くて、廊下と同じような通路
扱いになっていた。メジャーコードをつま弾いて、異性
について語り合うために、ボーイスカウトたちは地下に
隠し部屋をもっていた。シーダー女子中学校のサマン
サって子が、僕がいまでも唯一覚えている名前だ。キャ
ンプファイアーのとき、僕たちの班長だったローレンス
は彼女に釘付けだった。パグみたいな顔をしたローレン
スは時々気まぐれを起こす。一度、僻地の森で僕たちが
夕飯を食べ散らかしていると、彼はおもむろにスウィフ
トの班の方にのしのし歩いていって、そっちでご飯を食
べ出したことがあった。そのときの見捨てられた感覚は、
母と喧嘩になって父が家を出て行ったときと同じくらい
鋭いものだった。今じゃ結婚して軍隊の団長をやって
る彼が、当時ラジオでしょっちゅうかかっていた「リー
ダー・オブ・ザ・バンド」のコードを探しあてて、それ

で僕たちは一緒に歌ったものだった。

　歌うことにあふれていた。お気に入りだったのは、プラスチックで保護された栗色の表紙がついた、バプティストの聖歌集。だけど教会が分裂して、神の言葉を憑依させたと騙って追放された牧師さんと一緒に教会を後にしてからは、貸しホールのステージの裏側に響いてくる合唱が好きになった。「主よ、愛します」、「主よ、ありのままの私を受け入れ給う」。これらの曲は詞とも音楽とも言えない何かだったんだ。それは、天国に到達するために繰り返す、原始的なパワーだ。牧師さん——もう一人のローレンス——は、今では世界中を旅して、娘を切断しては元通りにくっつけるマジックショーを行っている。

　僕は歌うことが好きだったし、ずっと歌とともに生きていけると考えていた。天使のような歌声だと誰からも称賛されたエルサが、そんな考えから自由にしてくれたんだ。僕は教会を離れたけれど、いまでもその考えが真実となる場所に手を伸ばそうとし続けているのかもしれない。

## THE CARTOONS I LOVED

The cartoons I loved to trace were *Conan the Barbarian*, wrists lashed with ropes to his ankles, and *Flash Gordon,* heaving under chains. Superhuman strength against unbreakable restraint.

Matt tied to his bed, that was the first time I was hard enough to penetrate.

To make Wolverine, the adamantine has to go in.

## 大好きだった漫画

　大好きで描き写した漫画は、『コナン・ザ・バーバリアン』——ロープで手首から足首まで縛りつけられている場面。それから『フラッシュ・ゴードン』——鎖に縛られて喘いでいる場面。「スーパーヒューマン」対「破ることのできない拘束」。

　ベッドにマットを縛りつけると、僕ははじめて彼を突き通せるくらい硬くなった。

　ウルヴァリンにさせるには、ダイヤくらい硬いものが入らないとならない。

## CHINESE WEDDING BANQUETS

Chinese wedding banquets are insufferable. Guests arrive an hour late at the restaurant slotted in a multistorey car park and dinner is served an hour later. Ten courses in clattering succession, from cold cuts to almond jelly. The couple, their parents, and the photographer struggle from table to table. The bridegroom is puffy red from too much drink. The bride, corseted in some heavy material, purple or salmon, not white which is the color of mourning, looks as if she is about to cry from tiredness. There is nothing charming in the scene. Worst of all, one or the other of my parents would get drunk—mother turning loud and coarse, father sullen—and we would have such trouble getting them out of the restaurant, down the lift and into a taxi.

## 中国の結婚パーティー

　中国の結婚パーティーには耐えられない。立体駐車場に割り当てられたゲストがレストランに辿り着くのは約束の一時間後、ディナーが運ばれてくるのはさらにその一時間後。コールドカットの肉から杏仁豆腐まで、コース料理が 10 皿、ガタガタひっきりなしに運ばれてくる。新郎新婦とその両親、それからカメラマンは、テーブルからテーブルへと移動するのに必死。花婿は飲み過ぎで顔を赤くむくませている。重くて固いコルセットを巻いた花嫁は中国で喪をあらわす白ではなく、紫か薄ピンクを身に纏い、疲労でいまにも泣き出しそうになっている。こうした場面に、素敵なところなんてまったくないんだ。さらに最悪なことに、僕の両親のどっちか片方は、決まって酔っ払ってしまう——母はうるさくてガサツになり、父はすっかり気難しくなる。それで僕たちは、二人をレストランから外に出して、エレベーターで下に運んでタクシーに乗せるのにずいぶん苦労したものだった。

## *DELICACY IN GAUDY THINGS*

The tip of a peacock feather. Porcelain spoons in a plastic bowl of ice kachang. The face of a four meter tall Guanyin. These are common examples of delicacy in gaudy things.

More uncommon is the delicacy not found at the edge of things, or in their finish, or at a height, but the opposite. Like the heart's recognition of a gold Rolex watch on a thick, hairy wrist.

When one could show up the ignorance of a loudmouthed enemy, but refrains, that is delicate too.

## 派手な物ごとの繊細さ

　孔雀の羽の先っぽ。カキ氷用のプラスチックボウルに入れられた磁器のスプーン。4メートルある観音菩薩の顔。どれも派手な物ごとの繊細さを示している。

　もっとわかりにくいのは、先端にも、食べ終わった後にも、高いところにも見つからない、対極の繊細さ。太くて毛むくじゃらの手首に巻かれたロレックスの金色の時計に心が温まるような。

　おしゃべりな相手の無知に対して、知らしめることもできたのに、そうしなかったとしたら、それもまた繊細なことだ。

## HE GAVE ME HIS NAME

Yisheng, my friend who wrote *The Last Boy*, told the army he is gay, and they categorized him as medically unfit for operational duty.

When I visit Singapore now, I sleep in my old bed, the bottom bunk of a dismantled doubledecker. The long pillow still stretches out there but it no longer hugs me back. The first man I brought home was an army warrant officer. He gave me his name but I cannot give you it.

A child then, Thomas migrated with his family from Vietnam to Singapore before settling in the United States. He in turn ran away from them by joining the Singapore army. Living in the barracks, he heard his officers entering their men's rooms at night, and sometimes in the day. Their shadows would flit across his window shutters. We were eating pork congee in the winter, in New York's Chinatown, when he told me this, certain of being understood without explanation.

I heard and saw nothing during my time. The deregulation took place within. When I watched surreptitiously my platoon in the showers. When a sergeant cocked a crooked smile at his map. Once, the guys carried up a popular mate, spreadeagled him in the air, and split his crotch against a pillar. It was done in jest but, oh, how excited everyone was, now I see!

## 彼は名前を教えてくれた

　イーシェンは『ラストボーイ』を書いた友人で、軍隊にゲイであることを告げると、軍事作戦への従事義務には医学的に適さないとみなされた。

　僕は今、シンガポールを訪ねるときには、上段を取り外した古い二段ベッドで眠る。抱き枕はいまでもそこに横たわっているけれど、もう僕を抱き返してはくれない。はじめて家に連れてきた男は陸軍准尉だった。彼は名前を教えてくれたけれど、僕から彼の名を明かすことはできない。

　トーマスはまだ幼いとき、アメリカに定住する前に家族と一緒にヴェトナムからシンガポールにやってきたんだ。それから今度は、シンガポール軍に加わることで家族から逃げ出した。兵舎に暮らしていると、夜のあいだ、それから時には昼間にも、将校が男たちの部屋に入っていく音が聞こえてきたという。窓のシャッターに彼らの影がひらひら揺れていたんだって。僕たちは冬にニューヨークのチャイナタウンで豚肉のお粥を食べながら会話していて、僕には彼の話の意味していることが説明なしでわかった。

　僕が軍にいたときには、何も見なかったし聞かなかった。自分のなかの規制が撤廃されていく時期だった。僕がひそかに洗い場で小隊の仲間たちを観察していたとき。軍曹が地図を前にして歪んだ笑みを浮かべていたとき。いちど、男たちが人気者の兵曹を運び上げて大の字にして、柱で股間を裂こうとしたこともあった。ちょっとしたおふざけだったんだけど、今になって、みんながどれだけ興奮していたのかが僕にはすごくよくわかるんだ。

## SHARP THINGS

A clever child.

Magnetite in a homing pigeon's beak.

Paper.

A hairpin bend. A nail clipper.

Cook Ding's knife. At first you see the whole ox. After three years the openings between the joints. Now seeing and knowing have ceased and the spirit moves where it pleases.

## 鋭い物ごと

賢い子供。

巣に帰る鳩のくちばしに挟まった磁鉄鉱。

紙。

ヘアピンカーブ。爪切り。

料理人ディンのナイフさばき。はじめは牛全体を見ている。三年後には関節の開口部が見える。そしてついには見ることも知ることもやめて、魂が望むところにむかって動くという。

## I IMPRESSED MY FIRST STUDENTS

I impressed my first students by reciting from memory "Nature's first green is gold." They were green, as was I, and so both received the soft imprint of those days the way bracken retains the pressure of the body that has since moved off.

Green is also camouflage. The thick No. 4 uniform. The myrtle green and fern green paint sticks applied to the face, neck and hands. The grasses tied to the helmet to break its shape.

Thinking about weeds, I recall an amusing senryu a certain dual career officer wrote after an Administrative Service dinner.

*The Prime Minister.*
All the officers shoot up—
a field of lallang.

## はじめて受け持った学生たちを驚かせた

　僕ははじめて受け持った学生たちを驚かせた。「生まれたての自然の芽吹きは黄金色」という詩を、記憶をたよりに朗読してみせたからだ。彼らも僕も、かつては芽吹いたばかりの緑だったんだ。だから、その頃の日々の柔らかな印象をいまでも享受し続けている。ワラビに載せていたからだをどかした後にも、それがかたちの変化を保ちつづけるようにね。

　緑色はカモフラージュでもある。ぶ厚い No.4 のユニフォーム。銀梅花の緑とシダの緑の水性ペンで顔と首と手を塗った。形をわからなくするためにヘルメットにも草を結びつけた。

　雑草のことを考えていると、僕はある共働きの役人が、行政サービスの食事会後に書いた楽しい川柳を思い出す。

首相には
役員みな挙手
ススキのよう

## THINGS THAT TILT

The Empire State Building in a snapshot. Rain. All the strokes of the letter W, upper or lower case. The fingers of the Bharata Natyam dancer.

To observe something tilt is not to be a part of it. An airplane takes off and I am pressed against the seat, towards the earth. I want to fly, which is why I bought the ticket, but my body obeys an opposite force. Leveling in the air, like on the ground, permits the attendant to wheel out the food trolley. This is necessary but not interesting.

Earthquakes. Turning forty.

*word*
*world*
*war*

## かたむいた物ごと

　スナップショットの中のエンパイアステートビル。雨。大文字か小文字でWを描く筆の運び。バラタナティアムのダンサーの指。

　かたむいた物を観察することは、その一部になることではない。飛行機が離陸すると、僕は大地にむかって座席に押しつけられる。飛びたいからチケットを買ったのに、僕のからだは反対の力に従う。空中で、地面にいるときと同じように水平になると、搭乗員が食事の乗った台車を押して来るようになる。それは必要だけれど、おもしろいことではない。

　地震。40歳になること。

## WHEN I GO HOME WITH SOMEONE

When I go home with someone, there is always the question of how I leave.

I untie his embrace and make to go, whether the sex has been good or not. This way, when he implores me to stay, his pleading eyes appear in a charming light, and his fingers tighten on me in a regathering of the seam.

I stay if I like him or if it is late. He presses me against his chest or turns over to his side of the bed, and we sleep till day outlines the curtain in chalk. How delightful when he kisses me with his eyes and slips my hand down to his morning hardness. Yet another kind of delight when he bounces up to make breakfast. Pancake with maple syrup mixes in with sweat and semen.

Or I leave, despite his plea. He asks for my number and writes it in a graceful hand in a moleskin diary. He comes to the door, unlocks it in the most reluctant manner, and promises to call. I walk back into the city, which wraps round me like velvet trimmed with stars. Sometimes it is charming if he will not leave me but walks me to the train station. It is definitely not charming when he leaves with me in order to do laundry.

A friend had the frightening experience of not being allowed to leave. The door was unlocked only after he had given him satisfaction. I do not say I want to be tied up but I observe that the men I like, they let me go.

## 誰かと家に行くとき

　誰かと家に行ったとき、どうやって帰ればいいのか、いつも疑問に思う。

　セックスが良かったとしてもそうでなかったとしても、僕は相手の抱擁を解いて、帰る準備をする。一緒にいてくれるように懇願されるのはそんなときで、彼の訴えかけるような目には魅力的な光があって、彼の指が再び硬く僕に絡んでジッパーをたぐりよせる。

　彼のことが好きか、時間が遅くなってしまった場合には、僕はそこに残る。彼は僕を胸に押しつけるかベッドに押し倒す。それから僕たちは太陽がカーテンにチョークで線を引くまで眠る。彼が僕を見ながらキスをして、朝のせいで硬くなった場所まで僕の手を下ろしてくるときの、なんと素晴らしいことか。それから、彼が朝食をつくりにベッドから跳ね上がるときの、また格別の素晴らしさ。メイプルシロップのかかったパンケーキが汗と精液に混じりあうんだ。

　そうでなければ、僕は相手の懇願にかかわらず、帰ることを選ぶ。相手は僕の連絡先を聞いて、美しい手の中でモレスキンの手帳に書き留める。玄関のドアまで来ると、まったく気のすすまない素振りで鍵を外して、連絡を寄こすことを約束する。僕は街にむかって歩いて帰る。街は無数の星たちがあしらわれたビロードのように僕に

巻きついてくる。相手が別れようとせずに、駅まで僕と連れだって歩くのが魅力的に感じることもある。洗濯をするために僕と別れようとするのは、間違いなく魅力的じゃない。

　ある友人は、立ち去ることを許されないという怖い体験をしている。相手に満足を与えるまで、ドアの鍵を外してもらえなかったんだ。僕だって縛りつけられたいとは言わないけれど、僕の好きな男たちがみなすぐに僕を出て行かせてくれるというのも、考えものかもしれない。

## *WHEN SOMEONE COMES HOME WITH ME*

When someone comes home with me, there is always the question of how I will ask him to leave.

If the man has a good ear, he does not need any cue, but leaves at a natural pause in the rhythm of the meeting.

If he asks to stay the night, I give in. I bring him out for breakfast in the morning, at the Irish diner now manned by Mexicans, so that he can hear the train.

## 誰かが家に来たとき

誰かが家に来たとき、どうやって帰ってもらえばいいのか、いつも疑問に思う。

もし相手の聞き分けがよければ、特に合図を送らなくても、出会ったときと同じ自然なリズムで去っていってくれる。

もしも夜のあいだいさせてくれと頼まれたら、受け入れる。朝になって、いまではメキシコ人たちが経営しているアイリッシュ・ダイナーに朝食を食べに連れ出す。そうすればその男にも電車の音が聞こえるからだ。

## WONDERFUL WINDOW

Jean François has a wonderful attic window. When I flop down on his bed, the ugly postwar houses disappear and ochre branches spring up to weave a basket of the sky.

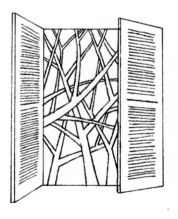

## 素敵な窓

　ジーン・フランソワは屋根裏に素敵な窓をもっている。彼のベッドにごろんと横になると、醜い戦後の家々は姿を消して、空が詰まったバスケットを編むために、黄土色の枝々が姿を現すんだ。

## HATEFUL THINGS

Caramel filling in chocolate. Hot rain all year round. Cold sea in the summer. A tulip browning in the spring. Babies. Pedestrians who hog sidewalks. Commuters who hog staircases. Small talk when I have not had a drink. Squeaky voices. They are especially unbearable when they read poems. Dates who talk about themselves the whole time. Dogma of any kind. It is even more hateful in the mouth of a handsome man. List poems. To be contradicted.

## 憎らしい物ごと

　チョコレートの中のキャラメル・フィリング。一年中続くじめじめした雨。夏の冷たい海。春に褐色になるチューリップ。赤ん坊たち。歩道を独占する通行人。階段を独占する通勤者。酒を飲んでいないときのおしゃべり。キーキーいう声。とりわけ詩を読むキーキー声には耐えられない。ずっと自分たちのことしか話さないデート。あらゆる種類の独断的な考え。顔のいい男が口にするといっそう憎らしい。リストポエム。反論されること。

## HER NAME WAS MARGARET

I sat with a dying woman in the hospice, and her name was Margaret. She taught me how to use fork and knife at a lunch buffet. She encouraged my writing by buying books for me. She brought me to Christ. Her name could have been Mother.

Now she was asking me to promise her something. What was it? What was it? I didn't want to promise it. In a voice frail and fretful, she asked me again and again to promise her. I'm dying and you won't do this?

A tree shot up from the broken ground. It raised a crown of shiny leaves. It rode as rigid as a scepter. Its name was Good and Evil. Its name was I Am Alive. Its name was Frangipani.

## 彼女の名はマーガレットだった

　ホスピスで、死を目前にした女性の脇に僕は座った。彼女の名はマーガレットだった。ランチ・ビュッフェでどうやってフォークとナイフを使うのか教えてくれたのが彼女だ。何冊も本を買うことで、僕の執筆活動を応援してくれた。キリストのもとに連れていってくれた。彼女の名はマザーだったのかもしれない。

　あるとき、彼女は僕に何かを約束するように求めた。なに？　なんなの？　僕は約束したくなかった。駄々をこねるようなか弱い声で、彼女は何度も何度も約束するように求めた。あたしが死にかけてるっていうのに、してくれないわけ？

　ひび割れた地面から一本の木が生えた。きらきら光る葉の王冠がついた。それは王権を示すように厳格に載っかっていた。その名を「善と悪」といった。その名を「私は生きている」といった。その名を「フランジパニ」といった。

## MOUNT FABER IS A MISNOMER

Mount Faber is a misnomer for the hill by which I grew up. It is not even the tallest hill in Singapore. I don't know who Faber is, but the word has always sounded delightfully like fable.

I went to a very small school on the hill. Radin Mas Primary School consisted of two distinct parts, the lower grades at the beginning of a long flight of stairs, the upper grades at the end. It was enough to teach one about large ambition and little achievement.

About the efflorescence of Singapore poetry in the last two decades, the critic Gwee Li Sui is right. It is not the result of cultural change, certainly not because of government programs. It has sprung up like wild flowers on a hillside, and it may die without altering the landscape. The best of us still aim to be major generals of a reserve army, pioneers of secondrate products, prime ministers of an island. The dreamier turn to poetry.

On every visit to Singapore, I make it a point—of what?—to walk up Mount Faber, going by the road that winds Toyotas and tour buses up. From the top I see on one side the public housing estates, intricate and useful, and on the other the featureless sea. Caught by the hand

46

of the hill, as if thrown there by a storm, lodges a boat. To the hungry eye it is a seafood restaurant. To the hungrier eye it is an ark. I look at the sea again and now I see the ships on the mauve horizon. I recite quietly a tanka composed a while ago:

Because this country has no mountains, we think highly of hills; look, we point to the peaks, where we can live.

# マウント・フェイバーは間違った名前

マウント・フェイバーは、僕が育った場所のすぐ近くの丘につけられた、間違った名前だ。シンガポールで一番高い丘でさえない。フェイバーというのが誰なのか知れないけれど、その言葉はいつでも 寓話(フェイブル) のように楽しげに響いた。

僕は丘の上にあるとても小さな学校に通っていた。レイディン・マス小学校は二つのエリアに分かれていて、低学年はひとつづきの長い階段のはじめ、高学年は階段の終わりに通った。大きな希望と小さな達成について生徒に教えるには十分な環境だった。

この二十年のあいだにシンガポール詩が花開いたことについては、批評家ギー・リー・スイの言っていることが正しい。文化が変化した結果ではなく、それに間違いなく政府のプログラムが原因でもない。それは丘の斜面にひょっこり咲いた野生の花々のようなもので、風景そのものを変えることなく死んでしまうのかもしれない。僕たちの中で一番優秀だったやつらは今でも、有名な将軍の補欠や、二流の製品のパイオニア、どこかの島の首相なんかを目指している。夢見がちだった者たちが、詩に向かう。

シンガポールに訪れるたびに僕が必ずやるのは、トヨタの車とツアーバスがぐるぐるまわっている道を辿って

マウント・フェイバーを登ることなんだ。てっぺんから、片側には、公営住宅団地が見える。複雑で実用的だ。もう片側には、特徴のない海。丘の手につかまれて、まるで嵐の只中に投げ込まれたかのように、一隻のボートが浮かんでいる。空腹を抱えた目には、それはシーフード・レストランに見える。さらに飢えた目には、それはノアの方舟だ。再び海に視線をやると、今度は何隻もの船が藤色の水平線に浮かんでいるのが見える。僕は少し前につくった短歌を静かに口にする。

山のない国だからこそ丘を思う　頂きにだって僕らは暮らす

# *CHINA*

It rained so hard that we canceled the hike for fear of landslides. Instead of tramping along the flank of Tiger Leaping Gorge, we visited Yufeng Temple, a Scarlet Sect lamasery at the southern foot of Jade Dragon Snow Mountain. The main hall was undergoing reconstruction, and so we climbed to the topmost courtyard to view "the King of the Camellias."

We were too late to see the thousand camellia blooms. The tree flowered in the spring for one hundred days, putting out twenty thousand blossoms in twenty batches. Without its tremendous bouquet, the tree was still an impressive sight. It was not very tall but held up a great canopy of twisty branches. It was planted in Emperor Chenghua's era in the Ming Dynasty, which makes it older than the temple.

If the tree were blooming, a close examination would show that it puts out two kinds of flowers, bigger pinks with nine pistils, and smaller whites with single pistils. The explanation for this miracle is that the camellia is not one tree but two. Growing at first side by side, they became so entwined through the years that they are now indistinguishable from each other. Voluptuaries of the sun and rain, they have fused into one in their joint pursuit of essential needs, outliving the generations of monks that tended them, displaying every year the hue of youth.

　雨がひどかったから、地滑りをおそれてハイキングはやめにした。僕たちは虎跳峡沿いを歩いてまわるかわりに、玉龍雪山南側のふもとにあるスカーレット宗派のラマ教僧院である玉峰寺を訪ねた。本殿はあいにく修復中で、僕たちは最上層に登って中庭から「椿の王様」を眺めることにしたんだ。

　幾千もの椿の花が咲き誇っているところを見るには、時期が遅すぎた。その木は春に 100 日のあいだ、花を咲かせる。20 の束に 2000 の花をつけるのだ。とてつもないブーケを抜きにしても、その木はやはり印象的だった。すごく背が高いわけではないのだけれど、張り出した立派な屋根のように曲がりくねった枝々が拡がっていた。明王朝のときに成化帝が植えた木で、寺院自体よりも古い。

　椿が開花しているときにその木をよく観察してみれば、二種類の花が見出せるはずだ。9 本の雌しべがついたピンク色の大きい花と、一本だけ雌しべがついた白い小さい花。この不思議な現象は、椿が一本の木ではなく二本であるということで説明されている。はじめは並んで生えていた木が長い年月のあいだに次第に絡み合って、今ではお互いを区別することはできないっていうわけ。日光と雨をこころゆくまで浴びて、彼らは互いを必要としあいながら枝と枝でひとつに合体して、何世代にもわたって彼らを愛でてきた僧侶たちより長生きして、青春の色合いを毎年見せつけているんだ。

## *THINGS SUBTLE YET POWERFUL*

A muscular back. The fragrance of shaving cream late in the day. The outline of summer lightning.

There are things subtle but not powerful, like a woman's voice. There are things powerful but not subtle, like a man's opinion. Then they meet and tumble, drunk, in bed, and Sei Shōnagon is born.

Winston prizes delicacy. In music he prefers the tone poems of Debussy to Beethoven's symphonies. I am drawn to strength, brimming but restrained by the lip of a cup. The restraint I learned from him.

The influence of a good teacher. That of a bad one. Freshly fallen snow.

## 微かでも力強い物ごと

　筋肉質の背中。一日の大部分が過ぎたあとのシェイビングクリームの香り。夏の稲妻の輪郭線。

　女性の声みたいに、微かで力強くない物ごともある。男性の意見みたいに、力強いけれど微かでない物ごともある。で、それらが出会って、転げまわって、酒に酔って、ベッドに入って、そうして清少納言が生まれる。

　ウィンストンは繊細さを大切にする。音楽の中では、ベートーベンのシンフォニーよりドビュッシーの音詩が彼の好みだ。カップのへりから溢れんばかりになりながらも抑制された力強さに、僕は惹かれる。彼から学んだ抑制だ。

　良い教師の影響。悪い教師の影響。みずみずしく降ってきた雪。

## *HAPPINESS*

I wrote this haiku for Kimiko's workshop:

An old man
walking an old dog.
Rain tonight.

Reading it again this morning with a great deal of self satisfaction, I remember the poem by Wallace Stevens "Description Without Place." My pleasure reddens into happiness.

## 幸福

キミコのワークショップのために、こんな俳句を作った。

老人が
老犬連れる
雨の宵

　今朝、自分で大いに満足しながらこの句を詠みなおしてみて、ウォレス・スティーヴンの「場所のない描写」という詩を思い出した。僕の喜びは幸福にむかって赤くなる。

## FIRST THINGS

When I fell in school after a rainstorm, I muddied my white shorts. I was terrified of looking as if I had fouled myself and so I tried to clean my shorts on the white columns that ribbed the walls. The stain not only stayed but multiplied.

The first time I entered a storytelling competition, I told the fable about a dog and the bone it stole.

I was thirteen when I published my first poem.

The first time I fell in love, I was talking to God. After Darren prayed for me at Lee Abbey, I could hardly leave his side. Away from him I was restless, scattered, insubstantial, a song without a singer. At Communion, I could hardly wait for the body of Christ to give each other the sign of the peace, when I could hold him briefly. In the New American Standard Bible, which I owned then, Jonathan loved David as himself. That was how I loved Darren when I turned twentyone.

I had to bring a date for the Administrative Service Dinner, and so I brought a girl out for the first time.

The first time I saw New York was like the first time I saw Oxford, although one was more like a movie and the other more like a book. Closing a book is harder.

I was thirtythree the first time I had sex. I was so excited that I could not come. I had to get out of the futon and go to the bathroom to lose it.

# はじめての物ごと

　暴風雨の後に学校で転んだとき、僕は白いショーツを泥だらけにしてまった。漏らしてしまったように見えることを恐れて、白いでこぼこのついた壁を使ってきれいにしようと試みた。汚れは消えないどころか増えてしまった。

　はじめてストーリーテリングの賞に応募したときには、一匹の犬とその犬が盗んできた骨の話をしたんだ。

　はじめての詩を発表したのは、13歳のときだった。

　はじめて恋に落ちたとき、僕は神さまに語りかけていた。ダレンがリー修道院で僕のために祈ってくれたとき、僕は彼のそばを離れることができなかった。彼がいないと、僕は落ち着かなくて、ばらばらになってしまって、実体のない、歌手のいない歌のような存在だった。彼をすぐにでも抱き締められることになったとき、聖体拝領でキリストの身体が平和のしるしを各々に与えてくれるのを待ちきれなかった。そのとき持っていた『新アメリカ標準訳聖書』では、ジョナサンはデイヴィッドを自分自身のように愛していた。それが、僕が21歳になってダレンを愛していたときのことだ。

　行政サービスの食事会に異性の相手を連れていかなければならなかったとき、僕ははじめて女性を連れて出掛けた。

　はじめてニューヨークを見たときは、はじめてオックスフォードを見たときと似ていたけれど、前者はもっと映画みたいで、後者はもっと本みたい。本を閉じる方が難しい。

　33歳で、はじめてセックスをした。あまりに興奮しすぎて、果てることができなかった。布団を出てトイレに駆け込まなければならなかった。

## AFTER THEY RETURN

After they return from field training, before they change out of their sweatstiff uniforms or muddy boots, the servicemen clean their M16s. They snap their rifles apart. They pull a steel brush through the barrel several times and several times more a strip of flannel held in the eye of the cleaning rod. They dismantle the bolt carrier group, the guts of the gun, to wipe the carbon off the bolt carrier. When the soot comes off, the firing pin is pure silver. Then the firearm is reassembled, the parts clicking into place. The steel body is brushed with motor oil and the buttstock blackened with boot polish. The rifles are returned to their racks, a chain is run through their charging handles, the showers hiss.

All this done with a fatigued swiftness still easy to recall now, so many years later, and so far away, sitting at my desk, writing. The speed and the exhaustion stay in the body, bright like a firing pin.

## 戻ってきたあと

　現地訓練から戻ってきたあと、汗まみれになったユニフォームか泥だらけのブーツを取り替える前に、軍人たちはM16をきれいにする。銃を身体から外す。銃身を何度かスチールブラシでふいて、さらに何度か、フランネルの布で洗矢を包む。銃の心臓部であるボルト操作部を取り外して、炭素をきれいに拭う。煤が落ちると、銃針は混じり気なしの銀色になる。それから銃器は再び組み立てられて、部品があるべき場所にカチカチはまっていく。鉄のボディは潤滑油で磨かれて、銃床は靴用クリームで黒くなる。銃は棚に戻されて、チャージングハンドルに鎖がかけられ、シャワーがしゅーしゅー音を立てる。

　疲れ切っているゆえの無駄のなさによって実行されたそのすべての過程を、いまでも簡単に思い出すことができるんだ。あれからすごく長い年月が過ぎて、すごく遠くにいて、こうやって机に座って執筆しているときでさえも。その速度と疲労感が銃針のような鮮やかさでからだの中に残っている。

## THE PLEDGE

School began day after day, as it still does, with the national anthem followed by the pledge.

We, the citizens of Singapore,
pledge ourselves as one united people,
regardless of race, language or religion,
to build a democratic society,
based on justice and equality,
so as to achieve happiness, prosperity
and progress for our nation.

It is quite without charm, this iambic self determination, except perhaps for the unintended link, through slant rhyme, of religion and nation.

Like a mantra, it is recited at every National Day Parade, when PAP MPs turn out in symbolic white, and the Opposition in motley. The Senior Minister, the Mentor Minister and then the Prime Minister also emerge in white, their faces impressive as icons.

The High Priest, the President of the Republic, is driven round the stadium to receive the praise offering of fifty thousand party clackers. After he ascends the altar, his batik shirt as colorful as garlands, he waves for silence, and the nation swells into the hymn 'Majulah Singapura'.

Right on cue, the heavenly sign appears, a giant Singapore flag, red and white, carrying a crescent moon and five stars. Suspended from a Chinook helicopter, the mantle flies slowly across the sky, its edges straight, its fabric fluttering in the strong crosswinds.

O, charming pageantry, that lends a body to abstract ideals. It moves me, this small nation's effort to make something of itself, though it infuriates me at so many other times. Together with the Singaporeans round me, I cheer the marching contingents and then the mass displays.

## かたい誓約

　学校は来る日も来る日も、国歌とその後に続くかたい
誓約と共にはじまった。今でもそうだ。

我らシンガポール市民は、
ひとつに団結した人民として自らに誓約す、
人種、言語、宗教にかかわらず、
民主主義社会を建設することを、
正義と平等に基づいて、
幸福と繁栄と、
国家の繁栄を成し遂げるため

　この弱強格による自己決定の詩は、おそらく意図せず
に宗教と国家とで韻を踏んでいるところを除けば、まっ
たく魅力を欠いている。

　人民行動党の地区議員は象徴的な白で着飾り、野党の
方はごちゃごちゃの色で着飾るナショナルデイ・パレー
ドのたびに、この誓約はマントラのように唱えられる。
上級相、内閣顧問、それから首相も白で現れる。彼らの
顔はアイコンとして印象的だ。

　共和国の大統領である大司教は、スタジアムのまわり
を運ばれながら、5000個のパーティークラッカーによ
る賞賛を受ける。花冠のようにカラフルなろうつけ染め
のシャツを纏った大司教が祭壇を登って静粛を求める

手振りをすると、聖歌「マジュラー・シンガプーラ（進めシンガポール）」で国家は波打つ。

　タイミングぴったりに、このうえないシンボルがあらわれる。赤と白で、三日月と五つ星をあしらった巨大なシンガポールの国旗だ。チヌーク型ヘリコプターから吊るされて、旗はゆっくりと空を横切って羽ばたき、縁はまっすぐに保たれ、生地は激しい向かい風を受けてぱたぱたと波打つ。

　ああ、心惹かれる壮麗なショーに、からだは抽象的な理想像へとかわってしまう。他のときには数限りなく僕を憤怒に駆り立てるのだけれど、この小さな国が自分自身で何か成し遂げようと努力していることには、感動させられてしまう。僕はまわりのシンガポール人たちと一緒になって、軍事部隊の行進とその後の整列の様子に喝采を送る。

# WHY I MOVED TO THE UNITED STATES AND NOT THE UNITED KINGDOM

When I walked into McDonalds in Welshpool, the floor sucked at my sneakers. The server would rather rib his friend who came in after me than take my order. He gave me a cheeseburger when I asked for a quarterpounder with cheese. He counted my change laboriously. The fries must have sat in the sieve since morning.

That was in 2002, when the Queen celebrated her Golden Jubilee, New Labor was losing its shine, and Nelson Mandela called Tony Blair 'America's Foreign Minister'. When I walked out of that joint, I had made up my mind to go where real power resided.

Since then I have discovered that the superpower does fast food badly too. That the corner where McDonalds is done the way McDonalds should be done is Singapore.

## なぜアメリカに移住することを選んで、
## イギリスを選ばなかったか

　イギリスのウェルシュプールのマクドナルドに入った
とき、僕のスニーカーに床が吸いついてきた。店員は僕
の注文をとるよりも、後から入ってきた友人と冗談を言
い合うことを好んだ。僕がチーズクォーターパウンダー
を頼むと、チーズバーガーを寄こしてきた。おつりを数
えるのにえらく苦労していた。ポテトは朝からざるに居
座っていたに違いなかった。

　2002年のことで、女王の即位50周年記念があって、
新労働党は輝きを失っていて、ネルソン・マンデラはト
ニー・ブレアを「アメリカの外務大臣」と呼んだ。建物
を出たとき、僕は本物のパワーが宿っている場所に行こ
うと決めた。

　それから、超大国〔スーパーパワー〕アメリカでもファーストフードは
ひどいってことがわかったんだ。マクドナルドでやるべ
きことをマクドナルドでやっているのは、シンガポール
の街角だった。

## THINGS OUT OF PLACE

A flute in a trumpet case.  Red wine on white linen. Sprays of heath in a blue bucket outside a Korean deli. A cheeky boy among mourners at a wake. A beautiful man married to a woman. A Singaporean in New York. The Singaporean in Singapore.

The moon in a lake.

## 場違いな物ごと

　トランペットケースに入ったフルート。白いリンネルに置かれた赤ワイン。コリアン・デリの店の外にある、青いバケツに入ったヒースの束。通夜の会葬者にまじった生意気な少年。女性と結婚した美しい男性。ニューヨークのシンガポール人。シンガポールのシンガポール人。

　湖に浮かぶ月。

## THE PUBLIC SERVICE COMMISSION

They have seen us all, these six men who interview the brightest in Singapore to decide on scholarships. Civil servants, military officers, and business leaders, they could have sat in that formidable row for thirty years, just as we, alone on the other side of the long table, are in a certain sense interchangeable. The idea does not diminish them or us.

But I am asking their support for changing me. I am asking for the Lee Kuan Yew Scholarship to become a poet. I explain it is time to develop more than factories, battalions and public housing, it is time to develop a language of our own.

They are not impressed. They can see through me. They know that I will quit Singapore for the States, that I am a queer one.

What they cannot see is that working in a rented room in Queens I write by the light of Singapore, a tall yellow streetlamp with its cloud of flying insects. Rallying my troops with Matisse's fighting words—to be a force that cannot be dismissed—I fear that, like my country, I am too small to survive. Even when I dream, like Keats, to be numbered among the English poets, I am making into an Abbey the mysterious power station in which my father worked for thirty years but I have never seen.

## 公益事業委員会

　彼らは僕たち全員を見ていた。スカラーシップを決める
ために、シンガポールでもっとも優秀な人間に面接する 6
人の男たち。国家公務員、陸軍士官、ビジネスリーダー、
みな 30 年間その恐るべき一列に座ってきたのかもしれな
い。反対側の長机に一人きりで座る、ある意味では交換可
能な僕たちと、ちょうど対照的に。その考え方は、彼らの
ことも僕たちのこともおとしめるものではない。

　でも僕は、自分を変えるための援助を彼らにお願いし
ているんだ。僕が詩人になるために出願しているのは、
リー・クアン・スカラーシップ。今は工場や中隊や公営
住宅よりも、自分たち自身の言語を発展させるべきとき
なんだと、僕は説明する。

　彼らの心には響いていない。僕を見透かすことができ
るんだ。彼らは、僕がシンガポールを去ってアメリカに
行くこと、僕が同性愛者だということを知っている。

　彼らに見えていないのは、僕がクイーンズの借間で働
きながら、シンガポールの明かりに照らされて執筆して
いるということだ。飛び回る無数の虫たちに囲まれた、
背の高い黄色い街灯。「おとしめられることのない力にな
れ」というマティスの戦闘的な言葉で自分の中の兵士た
ちを奮い立たせながらも僕は、自分の国と同じように、
生き延びるには小さすぎるのではないかと怯えている。
たとえキーツのように英語詩人の中に数えられることを夢見て
いるときでさえ、修道院の姿を父が 30 年間仕えたミステリア
スな発電所へと置き換えてしまっているんだ。僕はそこを一
度も見たことがないのに。

## JAPANESE THINGS

Tamagotchi. The highest standard of living in Asia.

A third language offered in secondary school, if you are good in English and Mandarin.

Comics illustrating love between men, created by women for women.

Hugging pillow, also called a Dutch wife.

His cock still inside me, the man answered a call from his mother in Tokyo.

Suicidal sects. Asymmetry.

After the Japanese occupied Singapore, they purged the island. Among the men shot at Changi Beach were donors to the China Relief Fund, men with tattoos, and Hainanese. The death toll is claimed by some to be 100 000. The Japanese claim 5 000. The truth is buried in between.

The Red and White Song Competition. Akina Nakamori.

## 日本の物ごと

　たまごっち。アジアで一番高い生活水準。

　中学校で、英語と標準中国がよくできる場合に与えられる第三言語。

　女性によって女性のために描かれた、男性同士の恋愛を扱う漫画。

　抱き枕。ダッチワイフともいう。

　モノがまだ僕に入っているのに、その男は東京にいる母親からの電話に応じた。

　集団白殺。非対称形。

　日本はシンガポールを占領したあと、島の粛清を行った。チャンギビーチで撃たれた者たちは中国救済基金への提供者であり、タトゥーを身につけた海南人だった。死亡者数は、100000 人に及んだはずだと言う人もいる。日本人は、5000 人だと言う。真実はそのあいだに埋まっている。

　紅白歌合戦。アキナ・ナカモリ。

## THE OLD CHINESE POETS

The old Chinese poets composed a poem after walking just a few short steps. The closest I came to this was to write a lousy sestina in my head after walking up and down the Bronxville park bounded on one side by train tracks and on the other by a motorway.

Walking in a cemetery is charming when there is light. In the summer the headstones can still be scanned at eight, or even nine o'clock. In the fall the leaves litter the graves and give them a melancholic look of being forsaken. The bare branches in the winter bring out the grittiness of the stones. In the spring, when the trees put on their freshest green and the birds are almost intelligible, the cemetery turns into a sculpture garden like the Tuileries.

The deepest darkness I know is the long night marches during National Service, the battalion strung out in a single file, scraping over the humpbacked ground, wading waistdeep across a river as black as tar, pressing through impenetrable thorn. The worst thing that could happen was to lose contact. All that kept the line together was the blue Cyalume straw on the back of the helmet of the man in front, and of the man in front of him.

It is so comforting to walk along a familiar path. The mind returns from observing, deciding, and judging to itself. It is like wandering out and walking home at the same time. Doing just that along the East River this morning, I made up this tanka:

The sun casts shadows, and so why am I surprised that love makes darkness, as if I am not in its way?

## 中国の古い詩人たち

　中国の古い詩人たちは、小刻みに数歩あるいただけで詩をつくった。それにもっとも近い経験をしたのは、下手くそな六行六連詩を頭の中でつくったときで、片側を線路、もう片側を高速道路で挟まれたブロンクスヴィル公園を行ったり来たりしたあとのことだった。

　墓地の中を歩くのは、明かりがあるときには魅力的なことだ。夏には、8時か、9時になってもまだ、墓石をしっかり見ることができる。秋には落ち葉が撒き散らされて、墓は見捨てられたかのようなメランコリックな見た目になる。冬のむき出しの枝々は、石たちの気骨を際立たせる。春になると、木々は一番鮮やかな緑を身につけ、鳥たちはほとんど埋もれて見えなくなって、墓地はチュイルリー庭園のような彫刻公園に姿を変える。

　僕が知っている一番深い闇は、兵役中の長夜の行進だ。大隊が縦一列になって、太鼓橋を引っかきながら、タールのように真っ黒い川を腰までつかって歩いて渡り、踏んではいけない棘を押しやりながら進むんだ。そこで起こるかもしれない最悪なことは、互いの接触を失うことだった。全員をつなぎとめているのは、前にいる男のヘルメット後部につけられた青いサイリュームの蛍光ストローだけ。その男にとっては、さらに前にいる男の光だけ。

よく知った道を歩くのは本当に気持ちが安らぐ。心が、観察することや決心すること、判断をくだすことをやめて、ただの心そのものへと戻る。まるでさまよいながら同時に家路を歩いているような感じなんだ。今朝、イーストリヴァーに沿ってそうやって歩いていたら、こんな短歌ができた。

太陽が影を投げかけるやり方で愛が生む闇に　なぜ戸惑うの？

## THINGS THAT QUICKEN THE PULSE

Hurricane warning. Running the hand through a man's thick hair. Merino wool cardigan. A wave of flamingoes taking to the air. Happening on Matisse's *Red Studio*. The thought of an approaching quarrel. The restaurant door opens, and lets in a draught.

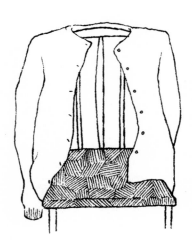

## 鼓動を速める物ごと

　ハリケーン警報。男性の濃い髪の毛を手ですくうこと。メリノウールのカーディガン。フラミンゴが空に飛び立つときに起きる波。マティスの「赤い部屋」に出会うこと。喧嘩が近づいているという予感。レストランのドアが開いてビールが運ばれてくる。

## HYBRID THINGS

Not only India but also Japan. Think, for a moment, of Zen.

## 混じりあった物ごと

　インドだけでなく、日本も。ちょっとのあいだ、
禅のことを考えてみて。

## ALL THINGS

All things diminish as they grow older, a friend of many years said last week. Even the expanding universe must contract. This morning, as I am boiling water to make coffee, his words come back to me, as sure as before, but smaller, because the whistling of the kettle takes up space. The steam was not so long ago a patch of snow. Love is what life boils into.

## あらゆる物ごと

　あらゆる物ごとが歳月を経れば経るほど縮小していくんだと、先週、長い付き合いの友人が言った。拡大している宇宙さえも、収縮に転じるに違いない。今朝、コーヒーを飲もうとお湯を沸かしているとき、彼の言葉をまた思い出して、前と同じように納得はしたけれど、その感覚は小さくなっていた。なぜって、ヤカンのピーッと鳴る音があたりを占めていたから。蒸気は少し前には雪の欠片だったんだ。愛は、人生が沸騰してできたものだ。

## *I MARK MY PLACE IN BOOKS*

I mark my place in books with bits of trash. A bus ticket in *The Ambassadors*. A grocery receipt in *Beyond Good and Evil*. In *Eleven British Poets* an old postcard from Singapore showing the airport tower at Changi. It occurs to me this morning while shelving my books that I mark my place in men with bits of my body. My dick in Tim. Big toe in Doug. Eric, whom I thought I was done with, has my left elbow. The beautiful boy last night who did not give his name has all of my fingers holding him open.

## 僕は本に読みかけの印をつける

　ちょっとしたものを使って、僕は本に読みかけの印を
つける。『使者たち』にはバスチケットで。『善悪の彼岸』
にはスーパーのレシートで。『イギリス十一詩人』には、
チャンギ空港タワーが描かれた、シンガポールからの古
いポストカードで。今朝、本棚を整理しているとき、男
たちに自分の体の一部を使って印をつけることを思いつ
いたんだ。ティムには僕の性器で。ドゥには足の親指で。
エリックには——彼ともしたと思うんだけど——左手の
肘で。名前を教えてくれなかった昨夜の美しい少年には、
彼をこじあけた僕の手の指すべてで。

## Translator's Note

　清少納言の『枕草子』の引用からはじまるこの本は、ま さに「ただ心ひとつに、おのずから思ふことを、たはぶれ に書きつけた」きわめて個人的な言葉の断片であると同時 に、シンガポールやニューヨーク、日本など様々な国の文 化や空気の匂いが自在に混ぜ合わされた、きわめて豊かな 色合いをもつ詩でありエッセイであり歌である。私的で濃 密な体験から、詩的で抽象的な思考まで、形式もテーマも 時系列も軽やかに飛び越えながら、「ばらばらの快感」とで もいうべき断片の心地よさを読者に与えてくれる。

　この本の性格を考えてみても、作者であるジーさんの生い 立ちや細かな情報を書き連ねるのは野暮なことであるように 思う。本書を読まれた方一人ひとりが、積み重ねられてい く断片の中から浮かび上がる書き手の姿を想像することこ そが、この本の大きな愉しみのひとつであるからだ。ただ し、彼が主にシンガポールで根強い人気を誇る気鋭の詩人 であり、これまでに4冊の詩集（"Payday Loans"、"Equal to the Earth"、"Seven Studies for a Self Portrait"、『マク ラノソウシ』）を発表しており、現在ニューヨークのブレア リー校で教鞭をとっていることのみをお伝えしておく。

　すばらしい作家の優れた作品を、このバイリンガル版を 通してより多くの方々に紹介できることを、たいへん嬉し く思っています。

坪野圭介